THE ART OF SCRATCHING

Shazea Quraishi was born in Pakistan, emigrated to Canada aged ten, and lived in Madrid before moving to London where she works as a writer, teacher and translator. A selection of her work was included in Bernardine Evaristo and Daljit Nagra's Bloodaxe anthology *Ten: new poets from Spread the Word* in 2010. Her first pamphlet, *The Courtesans Reply*, was published by flipped eye in 2012, and is being adapted as a play. *The Art of Scratching* (Bloodaxe Books, 2015) is her first book-length collection.

Shazea Quraishi

THE ART OF SCRATCHING

BLOODAXE BOOKS

First published 2015 by
Bloodaxe Books Ltd,
Eastburn,
South Park,
Hexham,
Northumberland NE46 1BS

www.bloodaxebooks.com
For further information about Bloodaxe titles
please visit our website or write to
the above address for a catalogue.

Supported using public funding by
ARTS COUNCIL
ENGLAND

Cover design: Neil Astley & Pamela Robertson-Pearce.

Printed in Great Britain by Bell & Bain Limited, Glasgow, Scotland, on
acid-free paper sourced from mills with FSC chain of custody certification.

ACKNOWLEDGEMENTS

Thanks are due to the following publications in which versions of some of these poems appeared: *The Delight-Tree: an anthology of Contemporary International Poetry* (The United Nations SRC Society of Writers, 2015), *The Financial Times, I am twenty people* (Enitharmon, 2007), *Images of Women* (Arrowhead/Second Light, 2006), *Ink Sweat & Tears, Magma, Modern Poetry in Translation, Ploughshares, PN Review, Poetry International web, Poetry Review, The Rialto, Sentence: a journal of prose poetics, Smiths Knoll,* and *Ten: new poets from Spread the Word* (Bloodaxe Books, 2010).

The Courtesans Reply was first published as a pamphlet by flipped eye in 2012

I am indebted to Manomohan Ghosh for his translation of the Caturbhāṇī, 'Glimpses of Sexual Life in Nanda-Maurya India', which inspired *The Courtesans Reply*. I am also grateful to Alain Daniélou's translation of 'The Complete Kāma Sūtra', an invaluable source of reference and material.

CONTENTS

You May Have Heard of Me

My father was a bear.
He carried me through forest, sky
and over frozen sea. At night
I lay along his back
wrapped in fur and heat
and while I slept, he ran,
never stopping to rest, never
letting me fall.
He showed me how to be careful as stone
sharp as thorn and quick
as weather. When he hunted alone
he'd leave me somewhere safe – high up a tree
or deep within a cave.
And then a day went on…
He didn't come.
I looked and looked for him.
The seasons changed and changed again.
Sleep became my friend. It even brought my father back.
The dark was like his fur,
the sea's breathing echoed his breathing.
I left home behind, an empty skin.
Alone, I walked taller, balanced better.
So I came to the gates of this city
– tall, black gates with teeth.
Here you find me, keeping my mouth small,
hiding pointed teeth and telling stories,
concealing their truth as I conceal
the thick black fur on my back.

Skyros

I live near the place with the honey.
It's always spring here. I sing
and cook, bare and brown
or in my purple dress.

In the day there are birds
with so many different songs, I can't choose
and at night, the brass shimmering of goat bells
leads me into sleep.

Maybe tomorrow I'll go
down the road with the purple rock and fig tree at dusk
to find the beekeeper's garden, dripping
with milk and humming.

Steps

Where I come from
we don't hang portraits of our beloved dead
to comfort us in empty rooms,
we hang their shoes, wrapped in gauze
sewn with surgical thread.

In my hall I've hung
my father's shoes, their soft leather
shaped by his strong
brown feet shaped by his journey.
I close my eyes and see my father

walking towards me.
As the day closes, I press my ear
to the air around me
listening for his footsteps,
his key in the door.

Darker than the Pansies

Darker than the pansies at the cemetery gate-lodge,
bottles of frosted glass filled with thick, pungent
liquids (lavender, pine sap, geranium, grass)
lined the top of the lower window sash, where they caught
the low light coming in – caught it and spilled it
on the cold, red stone of the kitchen floor,
so there appeared to be pools of liquid around her feet
as she stood with her hands in hot, soapy water,
thinking of the time she jumped into the pond in Hawley's field
and how the cold, green water filled her nose and ears
and closed over her head.

A Portrait

The husband makes a house:
the walls don't meet, there are gaps
in the floor but it houses them –
husband, wife, daughter, son.
　　　It is a house of skin.

　　*

At night, while the family sleeps
the husband carries the house on his back.
Sometimes the boy wakes on the floor. The girl dreams she is flying.
The wife sleeps soundly but weeps
on waking to disarray.

One morning before dawn
as he sets the house down
the husband feels a tearing in his shoulder.

　　*

Husband and wife stand in a field
– light pours on the husband, pours out
from his skin, his golden hair.
The wife is darker – the artist has painted lines on her face
that won't appear for many years.

Coke and Other Lies

When I look in the mirror I see the wrong face. My sister's hair shines like a summer lake with swans, and when she speaks, it's like those gusts of air you get in the spring, smelling of green. Since he left, Mom's lips have no colour and she reminds me of that albino kid who packs groceries at Doug's Mini Mart. She cries on the foldout couch. I stroke her hair. There, there.

My sister wraps her hair around Coke cans when it's wet, so when she takes it out, it looks like in the movies. Mom says she's wasting her time.

You know the man who sweeps up after the show? He said my eyes were the green of the pond at the end of his garden. He said, Come, see.

Mwanza, Malawi

I am Edith, I am eight.
I have two brothers, Jomo
and David. When we are hungry
my mother holds us close
with her body and her eyes.
Some nights I dream the same dream
– my mother covered in flies.

I jump out of the dream
leaving my mother alone
in the dark and the heat.
This happens again, again,
until dream-me holds her eyes open
puts one foot in front of the other
– goes like this to my mother
because of how much she hates flies –

and reaching her sees
a fine, black shawl covers her
with shiny, black beads
running over her like rain...
             and my mother is sleeping
             in the cool of its shade.

Story of a Small Block of Flats in Elephant and Castle

November 2007

January 2008

6am

dark	dark	light	dark
light	dark	dark	dark
light	light	dark	dark
dark	dark	dark	dark

6am

dark	dark	dark	dark
light	light	dark	light
light	light	light	dark
dark	dark	dark	dark

5pm

dark	dark	dark	dark
light	light	light	light
light	light	light	light
dark	dark	light	light

5pm

dark	dark	dark	dark
light	light	dark	dark
light	light	light	dark
dark	dark	dark	dark

11pm

light	light	light	light
dark	dark	light	dark
light	light	light	dark
light	dark	dark	dark

11pm

light	dark	light	dark
light	dark	light	dark
dark	dark	light	dark
light	light	dark	dark

Winter

He is an excellent swimmer,
jumping in the water like a dog, or sliding in backwards.

He keeps his eyes open and holds
his breath, staying under for 2 minutes at a time.

When he emerges, he shakes
the water from himself before it freezes.

His skin is dark under his white fur
which stores heat.

He is solitary, but sometimes
in February, he joins others to feed.

He is strong, patient and cunning.

He teaches boys how to be men;
that to be a man is to be a successful hunter.

He waits until they come close, or stalks them
on ice, spending much of the long winter out of sight.

He goes for the young ones
because they're small and slow.

The Drowned Sailor

I

In Norse the name means corpse whale
because its mottled, greyish
appearance suggests a drowned sailor.
Often feeding on fish

at depths of 1500 metres
under dense pack ice,
narwhal is found in Arctic waters.
The first year of a male's life,

his left tooth grows out, twisting
into a helix. This tusk,
ten feet in length, is used for jousting
or channelling sonar pulses.

Little is known about this whale
but there are stories.

II

Returning each year to the bay
where he drowned within sight
of his house, he saw his wife pale,
marry again and brighten.

Later, lonelier still, he saw
two boys who weren't his
(such fierce, sweet explosions) grow
into men, tender as trees.

Again and again he was drawn,
again turned away.
He saw her black hair that fanned
on the pillow, dull and grey.

One moonlit night towards the end
of her life, in a dream
he went to her and felt her hand
on his neck... such warmth.

Singularly Calm, Rather Wise

They line up – good, clean children –
from tallest to smallest. The cupboard can't confine
their implacable gazes – they question your
moving, breathing presence. Coloured lights
from the prism in the window veil them in
forget-me-not blue, green-gold, jellied
cherry. They listen. They believe rules
are there for good. The smallest two resemble
the girls next door. Silence presses – a silence of graves –
and you want to leave, you want them to be
like other children, noisy, grass-stained – not this metaphysical
existence, this sad patience, this endurance of mules.

True story

The woman who was not me sat down in the chair indicated by the doctor. She started to speak and proceeded to flow into the crevices and folds of the rough brown fabric of the chair, stopping just short of ending up at the good doctor's feet.

The doctor, whose name was Anne, put out her hand to place it on the woman there, and said how she liked to think of all the mothers alone at home all over the world, as hundreds of thousands of little lights shining in the dark.

The Wooden Family

Alone at home my husband
calls me, tells me he's painting
a wooden family. He says
he misses us but I can
tell he's captivated by
the wooden wife: she's mild as

a mail-order bride; all day
she gazes at her wooden
husband, all night she cannot
close her adoring brown eyes.
But the wooden children scare
him. The girl's too quiet – she

has nothing to ask or say.
The baby doesn't cry or
babble. He looks and he looks.
I kiss my husband at the
airport, and we are shy as
strangers, the children like goats

butting our knees. I say he's
pale – he says it's too much sleep.
When we get home, our red house
has shrunk and filled with sawdust.
Eager to meet the family
I'm appalled by the wooden

husband. His hair is ginger,
he's wearing a shirt I hate
and he's baring his teeth – he
looks insane. His wooden wife

is lovely if you ignore
the way her head narrows at

the top. She has my eyebrows,
her red lips shine and she is
wearing a green dress that was
mine. I hold the girl in my
hand. She's serene and pink, her
hair smooth against her head. She's

so still, and she wants nothing.
The baby is gorgeous with
his enormous eyes and his
succulent mouth, but he's too,
too tiny – he will be lost
in this world of sudden holes

in the floor and so many
sharp edges to damage him.
I know what this family means
to my husband, but all I
can say is, Why's her head so
pointy, and what's wrong with him?

Isn't he happy with his
wooden life and his family?

All This Time

I've been living the wrong life.
I stepped out to bring in the milk
15 years ago

and now I see
I'm in the wrong house.
Who is this man

with the plaster dust on his hands?
What are these children doing in the kitchen?
The boy is skinny, smells

of goat, mixes Cheerios
and raisins in his cereal bowl. The girl
reminds me of a jug

my mother had,
the china so fine, the milk shone
a blueish light through it.

Where are my bright
skirts, my heavy silver rings,
the red in my hair?

Cape Town

My brother Luc at sixteen
is almost a man
and bigger than daddy

but when he cries in sleep
he sounds just like
the skinny boy he used to be.

He has this dream
of walking on an empty road at night
and looking back

he sees our mother run out of a house
her hair crazy.
He can't move

can't speak
can only watch
as the dark swallows her

head-first
down to the white socks
on her shoeless feet.

      I hold him then, say
      Hush, Luc,
      it's just a dream.

Fallujah, Basrah

A poem in four voices

Rahim

Oh my son

Let my love
cushion the weight of your head.

Let me take your hurt
   I will hold it

while you rest
I will fold it into my body.

Sleep, my angel,
my flower, my brave, sweet boy.

> [*Child with extreme hydrocephalus – deformity of face, body
> and ear – and defects of cerebral nerves.*]

Sabir

I dressed him in a long white shirt
with a blue bird embroidered over the heart
and placed tiny white mittens on his hands.
Born with thick black hair
like his father, he was almost
so beautiful, almost perfect
as we had imagined him.

> [*Born without eyes*]

Farrah

Where is my baby girl,
the one I dreamed?
I long for sleep
to return her.

> [*Extreme hydrocephalus. The line running down the right
> side of the head would appear to show that potentially two
> heads were forming.*]

Anah

> [*It isn't clear what has happened to this child.*]

29

My Mother's Embroidered Apron

I am lost in my mother's apron –
green parrots drip from the trees,
a peacock brushes past me
pulling its clockwork tail of children's dreams.
I breathe in the heat of cinnamon,
the fug of yeast. My mother's voice
fills me like smoke and her stories
lift me – I rise like a yellow balloon,
my feet, white ribbons trailing in the long, wet grass.

Gold

I crossed the land with my small
gold baby. I had only my skin
which hung from me in folds, to wrap him in,
only my hands to cover his miraculous feet.
We came to a forest where the trees had faces;

there was a loud ticking and the smell
of waiting – dry, leafy.
I thought of his soft heart, the blood like finest embroidery
running through his body, and I was heavy
with the knowledge of animals in the forest –

the claws and eyes, the beaky hunger.
My baby stirred and the trees leaned closer.
I walked till I came to a wall of grass
reaching over my head. Then I heard
a shushing that calmed me, though

it could have been wings beating or knives
slicing the air. The grass
parted, like a sea parting
and my baby's breath on my skin
       was the wind in our sails.

THE COURTESANS REPLY

How wonderful is the supreme beauty of Kusumapura!
Here between the rows of houses the streets are well-watered,
well-cleaned, and are scattered over with flower-offerings great and small...
Daughters of courtezans, the beauty of whose lotus-like faces is being drunk
by the eyes of all people, are gracefully walking up and down,
it seems, to bestow their favour on the thoroughfare.

FROM *The Ubhayābhisārika*
translated by Manomohan Ghosh

Tambulasena

In the beginning
my whole body was covered with skin
hard as rock. Then he came

and his mouth
running over me was a river, cool and quick
with small silver fish.

Night after night
he shaped me,
smoothed me down

to velvet
bones.

*

Now I bathe while he watches,
eyes fireflies
on my skin.

I bend over,
my hair between us
a curtain of water.

I let him towel me dry,
his strokes soft... then brisk,
a cloth shining a lamp.

Water drips down
my back. He grasps my hair
and climbs.

The Sixty-four Arts

Of pleasant disposition,
beautiful and otherwise attractive,
master of sixty-four arts including
music, dancing, acting, singing,
the composition of poetry,
flower-arrangement and garland-making,
the preparation of perfumes
and cosmetics, dress-making, embroidery, conjuring,
sleight of hand,
logic, cooking, sorcery, fencing
with sword and staff,
archery, gymnastics, carpentry,
chemistry, architecture
and mineralogy,
the composition of riddles, tongue-twisters
and other puzzles, gardening, writing in cipher,
languages, making artificial flowers
and clay modelling,
training fighting cocks, partridges
and rams, teaching parrots and mynah birds to talk...

> Such a courtesan will be honoured by the King, praised
> by the learned, and all will seek her favours
> and treat her with consideration.

Vanarajika

speaks of the eight varieties of nail marks

Using the nail on my middle finger
I mark his neck
with a half moon, on the place
I like best
to kiss.
A sign of my devotion.

On his lower belly, I leave
a circle.

Often I trace a short, straight line
on his chest
his belly
his back.
The dash.

Lightly, he touches my cheek
giving me gooseflesh
then marks me with his thumb
deepening the scratch with the other fingers.
A knife stroke.

On my buttocks
a mark resembling a lotus leaf.

The peacock's claw is for me alone.
The hare's jump even more.

The tiger's claw
he traces under my breast
binds me to him.

Ramadasi

Return
to me, beloved
and take me on your lap.

Undo my braid
stiff
as buffalo horn

and draw your
fingers
through my hair.

Untie my belt, open
the silk cloth
covering my waist,

let my oiled limbs, my
perfumed skin
envelop you

as the rose
swallows
the bee.

Sukumarika

to Ramasena

My dearest, my life,
moon to my night,
remember our happiness?

Recall, if you can,
the equal kiss, *Sama*
and the pressed kiss, *Pidita*.
Aschita, the devouring kiss
and *Mridu*, the delicate kiss.
Also, the inflamer
the kiss of encouragement
the awakening kiss
the vagabond, the joyful
kiss, the vibrant one
the bowed kiss, the twisted kiss and
the satisfied kiss.

Have you forgotten
the taste of my mouth
sweetened with betel?
My garments, outer and inner,
white as milk.
The sound of my bangles
during love, their silence
in sleep.

Remember my lips
nibbling
pinching
kissing

browsing
sucking the mango
devouring.

Remember
the way I make you feel
– like twenty men –
and in your hands
my painted feet.

The Days of Chandragupta Maurya

were split into sixteen hours
of ninety minutes each.

In the first, he arose
and prepared himself by meditation;
in the second, he studied
the reports of his agents
and issued secret instructions;
he met with his councillors in the third hour
and in the fourth, attended to state
finances and national defence;
in the fifth, he heard the petitions
and suits of his subjects.
In the sixth hour, he bathed,
dined and read religious literature.
In the seventh hour, while he made official appointments,
he received taxes and tribute.
In the eighth, he met his council again
and heard the reports of his spies and courtesans.
The ninth hour was devoted to relaxation
and prayer,
the tenth and eleventh given to military matters
and the twelfth to secret reports.
In the thirteenth hour, the king indulged
in an evening bath and a meal
and for the next three hours he slept
            but never in the same bed twice.

Priyangusena

speaks of the Keeper of the King's Zoo

He is not like other men.
He prefers me unperfumed,
likes to watch me

remove hair flowers,
undo the *rasana*
around my waist.

In the morning I am porcupine,
at night, *Dhole*,
four-horned antelope.

He tells me secrets
of the *Nilgai*, its fondness
for almonds,

how the *Chinkara* leaps
the palace walls
and back again.

Ratisena

to Chandragupta

While you sleep, I take
your white shirt
from the unpainted chair,
smoothe it with my hands
the way I smooth
      the tiredness from your body
            pressing my self against you.
                Shh...

Let me take your worries,
your secrets – those sharp
small stones you carry
with you always.

I know you have women half my age
– I see them in the street, swaying
like long grass, their saris
concealing slim legs
that circled your waist.

Are you my King
or the boy I met at the well
so many summers past?

I watch you sleeping;
my small bed cradles you,
my only child
my only man.

Messenger

Malatika remembers you.
Her passion, hundred-petalled,
grows and grows, eclipsing all flowers
in her mother's garden: lotus, marigold,
raat-ki-rani, rose.

Each day she strokes her skin
with perfumed oil,
each day adorns her self
with pleasing things.
And as she walks, thinking of you,
her ankle-bracelets sound,
a hundred tiny, silver bells
trembling.

Madhavesana

Once more this
pressing of bodies, his desire
beating against me as the eagle's wings
against the air that lifts him up, up.

My body has learned to soften
and bend, but my heart
like a child who will not listen, clings
to a soft, worn thing.

After I have washed the sweat
and trails of saliva from my skin,
I stand at the open window,
let the breeze dry my face.

Pradymnadasi

on biting

When he gave me the discreet bite on my lower lip
I sighed with disappointment
knowing his mark would fade.

The coral jewel bite he bestowed on my left breast
and then the right. Around my throat
he placed a necklace of gems.

I will wear no ornaments today other than kiss
marks on my ears, filigree
bites on my hot, hot cheeks.

Before he left, he gave me the bite I like best:
the nibbling of the wild boar.
        And so, he knew I would wait.

Sondasi

I smile slow as honey

offer him
my pollen-dusted breasts.
I press my nose to his skin
smell Varunika on him.

   Wait

the word a caress
I undress him
– the first time I have done this.

   *   *

The next day
she is not with him.

I seat him on the low, green chair
move in his lap
put my mouth to his ear:

   Tell me what you do with her

He answers
and I show him
the flame lit inside me.

* *

Varunika,
queen of forests.

Her teeth
marks on his lips,
her nail marks on his back,

       her love note to me.

    * *

A dark pink flower falls
from her hair as she passes
– I hold it carefully in my hand: five petals,
one scattered with small, dark markings.

Opening it, I stroke the velvet
inside – eleven stamens raise
their pollen-tipped nubs
to the tip of my tongue.

Devadatta

I'm summoned to the jasmine terrace
where he waits
reclining on the large, low bed
draped in blues and reds and oranges.

He's with Sondasi's servant girl
– her gaze is lowered, his
rests on her breasts, where a blush blooms
above her open blouse.

Her waist is a handspan, her hips
high and wide.
During the love act, he moves my legs
to one side

so she will see as he enters me.
He doesn't look at me
but over my shoulder, watches her
small, heart-shaped face.

Carandasi

Tell me I am necessary for you like sleep,
not like opium which carries forgetting,
or pleasant as a breeze
scented with jasmine.

Tell me what you see
behind my art, my bright cloth.
Look into my face and show me.

Tell me what you read in books
and hear in coffee houses,
at wedding parties. Teach me.

When our tired, gladdened bodies
drift onto the bed,
kiss me like a husband
and spread over me an endless blue wing...

Anangadatta

Dreams I have

The peaceful routine of household chores:
    sweeping the floors of the house,
        sprinkling water on the yellow earth outside the door.

Cooking my husband's food,
    anticipating his pleasure.

Feeding sweet, milky pudding to my child.
    Sewing a button on my husband's shirt.

To spend the whole night dreaming,
    my child pressed against my back,
        my husband's breath in my hair.

Epilogue:
in which we explain a few things

How can scratching and biting, even if they are painful, create pleasure?

Just as a whip
when used by the charioteer,
makes horses mindful of speed,
so the use of nails and teeth
during intercourse
engross the heart in the pleasure of touch.

Tell more of the art of scratching

When a man sees, even from afar,
nail marks on a girl's breasts,
he feels interest and desire for her
even without knowing her.

And it often happens,
when a woman sees nail marks
on the various parts of a man's body,
her spirit awakens
       and takes her to him.

How is a courtesan to choose?

Here is a list of men to be avoided:
        Those with tuberculosis,
        with worms in their excrement,
        with bad breath,
        in love with their wife,
        coarse in word,
        brutal,
        cruel,
        abandoned by their parents,
        insensitive to praise and insult,
        immodest,
        frequenting enemies for hope of gain...
        Also one who is a thief,
        an idiot
        or one who practises magic.

The Years

10

Clifton Road, Karachi. I pray to God to change me to a boy so I can climb trees and get my clothes dirty.

My father tells us we're moving to Canada. I can't wait – it's going to be like Disney movies: houses with porches and grass all around, sidewalks to cycle on, tree-lined streets.

11

Fleetwood Crescent, Bramalea. All the streets around here begin with F. There are hundreds of houses and not many trees, but we have bunk beds, chores and wall-to-wall carpeting.

I have a new friend called Terry; her hands are pale as her white shirt. She has three sisters – Rita, Shirley, Patsy – and an endless supply of chips with dip. Her brother Michael says Hi, then stays in his room smoking.

Terry's parents are kind and they're like people on TV.

12

My favourite chores are vacuuming and making my bed. There is so much TV, my brothers and I don't talk about our ugly new names.

You've got a weird accent.
Did you live in a hut made of straw?

My father gets a new job with Mattel and brings home Slime.

13

In the winter, on the way to school we take off our snowsuits, stumbling into drifts, our stiff jeans thawing all morning.

One day, three boys surround Terry, their words like spit on her face. They don't see me where I've bent down to get a stone out of my shoe.

14

Tim Newman. I follow him unseen, my heart thudding in my flat chest. He is like the songs, his hair is feathered. I buy two copies of the school yearbook to cut out his picture to keep.

> *If you didn't hang around so much with Rajini Malhotra, most people wouldn't know you're a Paki.*

I know how he'd smell if I got close. Clean, minty.

15

We move to the country – my father's dream. At Erin High everyone smokes weed, my new friends call me Brain and cheat off me. At home I cry to get 98% on my spelling test.

Every morning the boys line the hall yelling out numbers or barking at the girls. A boy in art class shouts *give face!* and laughs as I wash out my tray. Next year I'll be sweet sixteen.

16

Every Saturday in the summer my father and brothers go fishing. They leave before light for Six Mile Lake and come back smelling of goat. My mother keeps finding fish heads in the freezer.

Walking one morning to babysit, a motorcycle passes me on the dirt road. I hear it slow and then a man is in front of me unzipping his jeans. I run and then I cry.

17

I'm desperate for modern languages, I tell the guidance counsellor. A yellow bus takes me to my new school in the city. The bus driver's name is Floyd; his unwashed hair and beard reach past his chest. The kids at the back of the bus smoke joints and burn the seats. Sometimes Floyd slows as we pass the chicken factory with the windows down. He can't say my name so he calls me Sophie, for Sophia Loren.

18

I read 'Are You There God It's Me Margaret', and 'Forever', tingling through English. At lunch with the cool Italian girls we discuss 'Do you swallow or do you spit?' I say I swallow because there's protein in it.

The stoners on the bus teach me to roll their joints. One afternoon Floyd drops off everyone except me and the girl who goes to a special school. Her straight black hair is always in her eyes. Floyd lets me drive the bus even though I'm scared I'm going to crash it. The road is icy and I keep confusing the brake with the gas. He keeps putting his hand on my bum.

My father says *Shaz, don't grow up so quickly*. I bury my head in his shoulder.

19

I start university. Boys notice me.

I discover drinking and indie bands like Change of Heart and The Jellyfish Babies. At midnight I go dancing with my friends at the Bullring which opens when everything else closes. I dance and dance and I am happy.

Weekends, my father takes me home and we talk in the car. He says my skirts are too short. I tell him I'm a communist.

20

May. My father is dead.
I'm not yet 20.

I Want to Tell You

It was a beautiful evening,
the light going
the colour of old gold,
trees leafing and blossoming,
my feet meeting the dirt road
as shadows lengthened.
I was thinking of the tree I planted last week
behind the house,
of dinner warming in the oven
       and the trout
       moving like memory
       through the still water of Six Mile Lake.

At Six Months

My daughter doesn't like people
she doesn't know, especially if they're men,
especially if they're dark.

This is embarrassing
considering my family,
the colour of our skin.

My brother comes to see her.
She takes one look at him and cries
until I take her off to bed.

It must be colic, I say, thinking
of his three boys, their kisses like bubbles
bursting on my cheek,

their little arms necklacing my neck
– what I wanted for him.
It makes me sad

my daughter doesn't see
my brother is the gentlest man. He
loves God, makes omelettes, silly jokes.

Later, after he goes,
I find his camera on the table
its one eye closed.

Garden, Night

I watch my father at the bookcase
fingering spines like keys
and guess at what he's taken down to read:
Wodehouse? Tennyson? Yeats?
The standard lamp throws shadows on his face
and he looks young, though it's been twenty years
and memories have taken his place.

Shouldn't he be more pale,
how ghosts appear in books?
I can't move, can only look,
the glass between us deep as a lake.
Moonlight. He turns.
Shadows fall like lace.

The Mummy of Hor

In this cave-like room, lamp-lit,
the Goddess Isis spreads her wings
across Hor's chest to protect him.

But that's not all:
the four sons of Horus guard his entrails
and the human-headed God Imset guards the liver
while Ha'py, with a baboon head, guards the lungs.
Duamutef, who has a jackal's head, guards the stomach,
Quebehsenuf, with a hawk's head, guards the intestines
and other Gods watch over his body
while sacred symbols protect his soul.

Hor's body, wrapped in layers of linen
and bound with black pitch
is here
and you are gone.

> I think of you
> on that country road
> when your heart stopped
> and your breath stopped...

> I think of you there alone.

The Beauty of the Swimming Teacher

The way he throws rings in the water
for the children to swim through;

The way he coaxes them under
pulls them along like ducks on a string;

The way the water shines around him
the children gleaming like seals;

How, at lesson end
they float like stars
        they shine.

Wild Fennel

Oh my sweet girl,
body outgrowing girl-thoughts
that bloom and burst...
At five, your loneliness was hard to bear
but now you seek its comfort –
behind the closed door, your thoughts
drift through the room, mauve smoke
tendrilling through the gap.

Once you covered yourself in leaves
your face showing. Now you swim through cold
mountain rivers, brown reed in the water,
your quietness everywhere
like the scent of wild fennel.

Sweetie Girl

I love to watch my grandmother eat
tarte au citron, battenberg,
lemon drizzle cake. Lost
in the feel, the taste,
a low moan escapes her.

Later, calling me
by my mother's name, she worries
they are planning to put her in a home.
      Don't go.
Holding my hand at the door,
she cradles my cheek,
calls me sweetie girl.

Turieno

She watches her son sleep
brushing away flies which return
to move again over his clothes
his perfect skin.
She draws the thin white sheet over his head.

Outside there are mountains
and the hermitage they walked up to
that morning. A bee buzzes
at the curtain
twice the size of bees at home.

That night it stings her husband
as he sleeps
– the next morning they find it
dead beside him
a small puncture between his eyes.

Eight days remain
of churches and mountain roads
wine and coffee
air bright with sound.

If only life could be
made of such moments
strung together.
Love balances on them.

She tries not to notice
age showing in her hands.

Roses

(i.m. Annette)

Your hair curls and wisps
around your face.
We hide weak smiles behind gifts of soup, ultra-balm tissues,
Olympic badges, Turkish Delight, garden figs.
> I stroke wild rose lotion over your hands
> (*how small they are, how tender*)
> and the smell of rose fills the room
> drifting out to the nurses' station.

Walking home through the park I remember
your daily walk around it, your pleasure.
The walled garden is closed now
while they smooth the cobblestone paths.
> No one will see this season change
> through its flowers.
> The roses will be going now
> or already gone.

Still Light

You picture your mother as a tree
– somehow that makes it easier –
a silver birch, undressing
unhurriedly, as though days were years,
while a fine rain plays
like jazz in her hair. She drops
her fine, white leaves
one by one. Her branches
are almost bare now. See
how beautiful she is against the darkening sky.

Cousin

You carry them on your back,
your muffled parents and her
soft, small children
as you carry your sister's body
wrapped in its white shroud
over the bright, stoney ground.

Now the brown earth pillows
her, holds her small body
in its quiet lap,
        rocks her to sleep.

Goodbye, My Loveds

We saw you slowly
  unhook
    your lighter self
      from the dear form our eyes clung to

  all those tiny hooks
    and you were so tired

You left us all behind
  children at home baffled busy
    with child-lives child-pleasure in gifts
  parents sitting greyly hand-in-hand
    husband (how small he grew)
      brother sister friend
  all your loveds

And your sister held your hand through the night
asking you not to go
  please   not on this day
    but you slipped away
      leaving your laughter
        small silver bell
          ringing in our ears

Notes on found poems

I

The source material for a found poem can be
any piece of writing whatsoever.

After the initial act of selection
may follow excision,
trimming,
re-arrangement
or even, to a certain extent,
re-writing.

Or it may be simply
a question of selection.
So be it.

II

The writer of found poems will require the following articles:

a. A hammer will be found most generally useful.
b. Stout and thin paper, and some of a soft kind
    for wrapping up specimens.
c. String, sealing wax.

III

Marcel Duchamp never tired of saying:
> *The most important element*
> *in a picture*
> > *is its frame.*
> *in a sculpture,*
> > *its plinth.*

Additional Notes

'Singularly Calm, Rather Wise' (22) uses words from Gwendolyn Brooks' poem 'The Children of the Poor' and employs Terrance Hayes' golden shovel form.

In 'Fallujah, Basrah' (28), medical quotes come from Ross B. Mirkarimi (The Arms Control Research Centre, from report *The Environmental and Human Health Impacts of the Gulf Region with special reference to Iraq*, from May 1992) commenting on photographs of extreme birth deformities experienced in Iraq and Afghanistan following bombing with DU ammunition. All names are fictional.

In *The Courtesans Reply*, the first and last lines of 'Carandasi' (48) are quotes from the poem 'Two stranger birds in our feathers' by Mahmoud Darwish. 'Epilogue' (51) employs found text from *Glimpses of Sexual Life in Nanda-Maurya India*, a translation of *The Caturbhānī* by Manomohan Ghosh (Manisha Granthalaya Private Ltd, Calcutta, 1975) and from *The Complete Kāma Sūtra*, translated by Alain Daniélou (Park Street Press, 1994).

'The Mummy of Hor' (61) uses text from the curator's notes for the Mummy of Tem Hor in Swansea Museum.

'Goodbye, My Loveds' (69) was the painter Arshile Gorky's parting message written in chalk on a crate.

'Notes on Found Poems' (70) uses text from the following sources: the introduction to Malcom Parr's pamphlet, *Found Poems* (1972); a footnote from The Metropolitan Police Services' Investigation of Fakes and Forgeries exhibition at the V&A Museum; a quote from Germaine Greer in the *Guardian* (30 March 2009).